CW01511998

# The Blue Armchair

John Froy was born in Yorkshire and grew up in the West Country. He went to art school, travelled widely, and taught English as a Foreign Language. He settled in Reading with his wife and daughter and set up a decorating business. He managed Two Rivers Press for a number of years. A prize-winning poet, author of four memoirs about his childhood, student, teaching and travelling years, his work has appeared in anthologies and journals. *The Blue Armchair* is his third poetry collection.

# The Blue Armchair

John Froy

TWO
RIVERS
PRESS

## Also by John Froy

**Poetry**
*Eggshell: A Decorator's Notes* (2009)
*Sandpaper & Seahorses* (2018)

**Memoirs**
*Waterloo Road* (2010)
*The Art School Dance* (2013)
*Teacher Squatter City Farmer* (2018)
*On Cocos Island* (2021)

## Also by Two Rivers Poets

David Attwooll, *The Sound Ladder* (2015)
Charles Baudelaire, *Paris Scenes* translated by Ian Brinton (2021)
William Bedford, *The Dancers of Colbek* (2020)
Kate Behrens, *Man with Bombe Alaska* (2016)
Kate Behrens, *Penumbra* (2019)
Kate Behrens, *Transitional Spaces* (2022)
Conor Carville, *English Martyrs* (2019)
David Cooke, *A Murmuration* (2015)
David Cooke, *Sicilian Elephants* (2021)
Tim Dooley, *Discoveries* (2022)
Jane Draycott, *Tideway* (re-issued 2022)
Jane Draycott & Lesley Saunders, *Christina the Astonishing* (re-issued 2022)
Claire Dyer, *The Adjustments* (2024)
Claire Dyer, *Yield* (2021)
James Harpur, *The Examined Life* (2021)
Maria Teresa Horta, *Point of Honour* translated by Lesley Saunders (2019)
Ian House, *Just a Moment* (2020)
Philippe Jaccottet, *In Winter Light* translated by Tim Dooley (2022)
Rosie Jackson, *Love Leans over the Table* (2023)
Rosie Jackson & Graham Burchell, *Two Girls and a Beehive: Poems about Stanley Spencer and Hilda Carline* (2020)
Gill Learner, *Chill Factor* (2016)
Gill Learner, *Change* (2021)

Sue Leigh, *Chosen Hill* (2018)

Sue Leigh, *Her Orchards* (2021)

Becci Louise, *Octopus Medicine* (2017)

Mairi MacInnes, *Amazing Memories of Childhood, etc.* (2016)

Steven Matthews, *On Magnetism* (2017)

Steven Matthews, *Some Other Where* (2023)

Katherine Meehan, *Dame Julie Andrews' Botched Vocal Cord Surgery and Other Poems* (2023)

Henri Michaux, *Storms under the Skin* translated by Jane Draycott (2017)

Kate Noakes, *Goldhawk Road* (2023)

Alistair Noon, *Paradise Takeaway* (2023)

René Noyau, *Earth on Fire and other Poems* translated by Gérard Noyau with Peter Pegnall (2021)

Ruth O'Callaghan, *Where Shadow Falls* (2023)

James Peake, *Reaction Time of Glass* (2019)

James Peake, *The Star in the Branches* (2022)

Peter Robinson & David Inshaw, *Bonjour Mr Inshaw* (2020)

Peter Robinson, *English Nettles* (re-issued 2022)

Peter Robinson, *Retrieved Attachments* (2023)

Lesley Saunders, *Nominy-Dominy* (2018)

Lesley Saunders, *This Thing of Blood & Love* (2022)

Jack Thacker, *Handling* (2018)

Robin Thomas, *The Weather on the Moon* (2022)

Susan Utting, *The Colour of Rain* (2024)

Susan Utting, *Half the Human Race* (2017)

Jean Watkins, *Precarious Lives* (2018)

First published in the UK in 2024 by Two Rivers Press
7 Denmark Road, Reading RG1 5PA.
www.tworiverspress.com

© John Froy 2024

The right of the poet to be identified as the author of this work
has been asserted by him in accordance with the Copyright, Designs
and Patents Act of 1988.

All rights reserved. No part of this publication may be reproduced,
stored in or introduced into a retrieval system, or transmitted,
in any form, or by any means (electronic, mechanical, photocopying,
recording or otherwise) without the prior written permission
of the publisher.

ISBN 978-1-915048-17-2

1 2 3 4 5 6 7 8 9

Two Rivers Press is represented in the UK by Inpress Ltd
and distributed by BookSource.

Cover image: *Mother and Child*, etching by Martin Froy, 1953
Cover design by Sally Castle
Text design by Nadja Guggi and typeset in Janson and Parisine

Printed and bound in Great Britain by Severn, Gloucester

## Acknowledgements

Thank you Myra, Elke and Clare for your help with the poems.

Thank you Stones Writers and Thin Raft poets for acute interpretation,
criticism and suggestion, for your ever continuing inspiration.

My thanks also to the editors of *Reading Poets: A New Anthology* where
some of these poems appear.

And to poetry avenues and venues everywhere, Reading's Poets' Cafe,
East Reading Festival, Fourbears Bookshop, Caversham and Ian Florance
in Hampton – thank you.

For my mother, Anne Wild

and thank you, Naomi
for being here
for listening endlessly

# Contents

# Blue Dressing Gown

A reply to the Poet Laureate, 2003

*Her face comes to me later in the night*
*in the belly-chewing hours around four.*
*I touch her laid out in the chapel of rest,*
*mother's misshapen nose, icy brow.*

*They made a death mask from that*
*to keep them alive in a way, to last.*
*How slow I was to work that one out –*
*you must wait till they die for the mask.*

*I found a photograph, took it to town*
*to enlarge. Now she sits in her armchair,*
*owl glasses and blue dressing gown*
*beside the unlit summer fire.*

*I wrote to the Laureate in light of day.*
*He said to keep on writing about her*
*to keep her alive in a way.*

# I. Looking for Her

# Mothers A B C

Are you adopted too? she asked
as I bought her book of poems.
No, but I had several mothers.
How come? How many?
They mostly began with C …
Tell me.
Well, there was mine, Anne,
then $c_1$, who also died,
the best of them.
But no favourites, right?
Right.
Then $c_2$ who disappeared so soon
and $c_3$ who's still here, not often seen.
I think there was a B for a while.

# As I Set Off for London

The gas holder rises at the end of the road,
there are still a few leaves blowing around.

You, I imagine, are this tall quiet woman,
handbag clenched, walking these drab streets often.

Or that fierce lady in a Burberry, pale
fawn, the very devil at the autumn sales.

After leaf fall came your birthday event,
usually a bit of a nightmare, wasn't it.

Dickensian, your mystery benefactor,
the cheque that came from Brighton each December

which drove you to such a spending frenzy
Christmas at home came to mean anarchy.

Mum, you were ill, we kids gave you such stick,
I must, I will, make some amends for it.

I can see your sketchbooks from the train,
studies of cows in fields, sheep in the rain

and people in waiting rooms, bus stations,
figures, faces of the human condition;

despite all the pain, I know, lifelong,
you never lost your sense of compassion.

I'll look for postcards in the Tate for you,
Bonnard, Chagall, a Gwen John cat or two.

# Quartet

## Her Bedside Lamp

Home-wired, it fizzed a bit.
Fitting screwed into a section
of gilt rococo picture frame moulding
mounted on the tarnished base
of a post-war art school etching plate;
the pleated paper shade, once white,
perched cocksure on incandescent bulb.
It stayed her side of the bed
after she was gone. On visits home I grew
fond of this quirky, slightly dangerous
creation of both her husbands:
the ornate moulding and copper of my father,
Woolworth's home lighting kit of stepfather.
It didn't survive the last clear out.

## Portuguese Figurine

Cheap clay thing on the mantelpiece,
she was Granny's, a century old:
hands on hips, jaunty proud,
a peasant girl and saint,
our Lady of Fatíma, we think;
hand-painted in that remote era
with red flowered blouse and lips;
cerulean skirt, cobalt sash, lemon
shawl to contain the rave of her hair.
Was this also her only child, Anne?
Her large feet bare like mine, a hole
in the head for the votive candle.

## The Russian Watch

Between links of its bracelet strap
like a tide mark or dirty fingernail,
the scurf of her skin, there since
she gave me this old wind-up thing.

Her sight so bad now she couldn't read
even the large pale twelve-hour dial.
*Here, it's a man's anyway.*
Peeled it from her wrist and felt for me.

I've thrown the tarnished strap away.
*Good thing too,* she'd laugh:
*get a new one, leather, smart.*
That laugh, too-loud, filled the sitting room.

## *Walk On By* on the Hitachi

It comes like a breath of her
four and a half years on
on her battery-dead radio,
Dionne Warwick singing,
the station unchanged
since that afternoon she switched off
and came downstairs. She would go in.
Temporary. Respite. She never came out.
Now the music has gone, gone
but fiddling with the dial ...
there comes a murmur of the background radiation
surrounding me since the big bang of my birth.

# Deep Ecology

We walked across the ancient land, you talking
of Gaia, our earth mother, in uncertain April

and of your family perishing in Warsaw,
your father who got out ... It began to snow.

*Each snowflake is alive, you know, loaded with bacteria*
*returning from the upper air.*

And we came to the village of Melbury Bubb,
a clock-stopped church tower under the hill,

looked for signs of green men on the Celtic font,
in a disused chalk pit found sea creatures far older;

a plant world in miniature clings to the cliff there
only growing as big as it dares, as fits its niche.

Snow swirling, we climbed the wood-crowned Bubb;
deer leapt away; we picked wild ramsons, just enough.

That's when you said, glancing to the east
you would've lived back then. Before the Common Era.

*When humans born small remained so,*
*when little was enough for us all.*

I saw a giant, barefoot, spreadeagled on the ground.

# Travails of the Colour Blind

*Like my new costume?*
Yes I do! Pinkish or greeny blue?
Where is it on the colour wheel?
*Turquoise*, she helped
on the island of the colour blind.

Then: *A London bus in country lanes?*
I was only four.
*He means double-decker.*
*He means his red is green*
*and what is the red we see?*

An artist father's dismay at my disability
was underscored with intrigue.

We did the Ishihara test:
irrefutable dots.
*It affects boys, rarely girls,*
*comes through in the X chromosome.*

I had orange and yellow perfectly,
I saw all the blues,
brighter reds, some greens,
many brownish greys.
Purple and turquoise were killers.

Didn't want to be a train driver anyway.
Pilot, surgeon or electrician.
Bad luck captain of the ship is out.

*Why not be a teacher of art?*
said a mother of Matissian colour vision.

*Just look at all the poppies!*
Where, where?
From the back seat of the family car
wind like waves rippled poppyless corn.
*You just see differently, and plenty!*

But I missed the spots on the backs of roach
lazing in the river on school nature walk
and Christmas holly berries – *so good this year!* –
were invisible to my faulty eye.

I added knowledge, intuition –
found those specks of red in mass of green,
identified the dabs in Monet's Poppy Field,
felt the painting in my own way.

# Mum in Colour

On the cool marble mantel, there
among thinned-out cards and china,
in navy coat and white silk square,
this rare photo of her in colour.

Arm around a squirmy daughter,
she sits on a gravestone in the sun,
at some country church in Pevsner
where they've come on a Sunday spin.

She looks straight into the Voigtländer
smiling with her broken teeth,
less concerned with the Perpendicular
than the graveside woman laying a wreath.

Her eyes I remember as all milky sheen
were then a clear grey-green.

# Complicity

I know the lump inside Frank's letter,
just as I know what he will say:
*... to wish you a really good holiday* –
one Temazepam from the kindly man
so I get some sleep before my flight.
He cuts his in half with a Stanley knife
with all his usual precision,
aware of his growing addiction.
Now we're colluders in her drugs
half a tab each at times of worry.
*Amazing, your mother,* he said from her chair.
*Constitution of an ox, your wife,* I concurred.
She was taking a dose that would kill us both
by the end of her shortened life.

# The First Time I saw My Father Blush

we were in his Commer Cob van
the two of us, I had the front seat.
A bobby pointed to the winder,
then stuck his head through the window
to ask why we're parked on a zebra.

I watched my daddy's ear go crimson
so adjacent to the policeman
but knew he didn't mean whatever
it was, he wouldn't break the law,
no, it was nothing worth blushing for
but I reddened with him all the same.

*

Then he started kissing me
eighty-five years later,
his last year on the planet.
Galantamine from snowdrops
and daffodils ('used by Homer')
had become ineffective.

We were watching dark matter,
twenty-five percent of the universe,
in his last small room in the Chilterns
and as I stood to go, he touched his lips
beneath the straggle of beard
to blow me a little kiss.

# Tight Connections to My Heart

i.m. MB

After all, my friend, we were born
in the same ward of Leeds General
three weeks apart in the post-war mist of '53,
we learnt when we met aged thirty-three.
And our mothers would both die young
in Devon. You looked to the future
more than me (yet are not here),
always wondering what next,
which walls and bridges would be built,
while I looked back.

I'll tell you about Frank back then,
a man I've loved as much as anyone,
how we met in the transfer –
from Bristol Temple Meads Station
with my father, deafened by the trains,
I travelled alone, aged six,
my tabby kitten mewling the whole way.
To find a stranger on the platform
at Taunton, and maybe we shook hands,
he took my case, left me the cat,
the woman beside him all a blur
seen as if for the very first time.

# Oakley Street Letter: Mother's lament

Anne writes home to her mother shortly before her breakdown
in 1958

Just to let you know my address and number –
the good clean house of a woman doctor
who lets to students, actors and singers
(no, they won't steal) down by the Albert Bridge.
You can hear tugs hooting into the night.
My allowance is sufficient for rent and food;
I can feel my way around the big city,
find a part-time job I like.

I'll visit the children in the cottage in April
when M is working here in London.
I saw him when he brought my things
and the plan remains the same:
trying to face up to the position
concerning the children.
I will see a solicitor to see where I stand;
I must take charge of them soon.
It all comes down to earning more
and keeping in touch.
I sent a telegram on E's birthday
and a doll's house is following.
It's off with M, it must be faced.
If ever there was doubt in my mind,
seeing him here made it quite clear
in the name of health and sanity
and the children,
it is better we separate.
So long as we face the bitter facts
there is no need for despair.
I can't manage a visit at present.
Is it possible for you to come here?

# After the Separation: Stepmother's lament

Adapted from a letter

I heard 'Mama', thought it was midnight and awoke.
Maria was holding out her arms to me,
light streamed from her eyes.
She called Anastasia Maria Catherine and prayed.
As such she was your little bluebird of happiness.
Beautiful phrases: how much she loved you and me,
and saying the lamb of God.
I cuddled her, of course, but cannot remember
her murmurings because of the Church Trial.

I returned her to the cot after hearing her first words –
I had not taught her to talk – and went downstairs.
It was midnight. I went outside. There was one very bright star
above the house. I gave her bottle when she had finished praying.
I had this performance every midnight for five nights.
I didn't know how to defend her.

It was on the pillow she had her affair with either you or me.

Then she was sitting up when I woke.
Difficult to see in the dark.
I saw cosmetics for five nights and heard the prayers
which like yourself were a miracle.

I do not underestimate the importance of cosmetics.
The light from her eyes echoed the blue flowers on her white counterpane.
Will you make the case?

# Two Mothers

Suddenly I feel the other
beside this burgeoning hedge,
lush meadow of buttercup, lady's
smock, elderflower in this heady month.

I was holding onto her skirt
toddling down the grassy hill from school
when a grass snake slid out in front –
harmlessly it crossed the path.

I'd robbed a sitting blackbird's nest,
it was too late to return the eggs.
We pricked those cold eggs, blew them out
made cotton wool nests for the shells.

Now the long daylight and sharp
sweetness of this fresh mown grass
have combined to bring me to A's grave
west of there, under Blackdown Hill.

How busy the cemetery in the evening.
It is possible after all to have two.

# The City Balcony

Only our breathing disturbs the morning.
I see how it changes, a way forward now.
Your smile as you arched your back and cried
altered for ever the framed photo
on the chest of drawers, besieging me –

how strange to move from one to the other,
from mother to lover, to come to you
so neat and fitting, so thrilling. I'll get
my knuckles rapped for calling you a kitten –
tiger more like. It's not that I want a frame
around you, just wonder why this burns so.
I ask myself why, just now.

A question half answered by another image
rising with the sun one summer in the city,
so young with someone who isn't my mother.
She suns herself on a rubber lilo, rubs oil
on the fine black hairs of her olive skin,
and I prance in through the glass doors,
poke feathers from a brown velvet cushion
through railings miles above the ground.
At last I lay my head on the soft secret mound
knowing it isn't where I come from.

Let's do this when it is warmer.
I want to climb back inside you
like in that Almodóvar movie we saw.
When I go down, kneel at the delta,
and you call out my name, pull at my hair,
I might find among many other things
where I was back then on that balcony.

# Dunnock in Spring

And when the weather starts to warm
he looks around these urban gardens,
observes a flick of her rufous tail,
appraises ruffled feathers on a branch,
and, let's face it, an available cloaca.
If need be he will share.

She meanwhile, already taken,
has polyandrously noted:
a fine voice, smart plumage, decent territory.
It will entail a sharp peck from him
to remove the other's deposit
before he can make his own.

Little can be done with hormones in birds
and for all our fine feelings, ours.

# The Red Balloon

after A. Lamorisse

High over the city
a long white cord is snaking down:
   *With love from Mummy*
   the book she sent
   when I was five
   about a balloon's flight and narrow scrapes
   through Paris cobbled streets
   until the ruffians caught and stoned it,
   burst it in stark black and white.
With a postcard kept like an old key
I can now put two together:
our parents' last ditch attempt
while the children were lodged in Sussex.
Ooh la la, silly mother,
all that dancing in Montmartre
where life was better than here.
   Then all the balloons of the city
   join together, burst into colour,
   and carry the boy away.

# The Gold in the River: Analyst's lament

She calls, delayed – a patient arrived
when she had one arm in her coat.
The patient thought she'd just come in, talked and talked,
and now the fish and chip shop's closed – which saves
the new car from grease for a while, she laughs,
before she cries at the things she has heard today.
So we tighten our belts and walk the towpath
considering the next step –
my friend always changes the future.
When we had them before, out of newspaper,
she told me how she dropped her wedding ring
from Chelsea Bridge and started again.
With so much gold in the river now,
there was a job for a diving detectorist.

# Scatterheart

She left the house flying:
wine untouched, glasses unturned;
scorched cotton in the air,
the cat collapsed on her cushion,
a Hummel score on the piano.
Everything she left for us:
nuts, chocolate, hot cross buns,
her fairytale tin of Gretel treats,
a plate and napkin each.
How she'll leave us all one day,
driving pell mell down some motorway
to another in need of a listening ear,
an oblivion I fear.

# First Picasso

The first Picasso I ever saw
was in the lav on the landing
of a tall old house with red-lead doors:
*Weeping Woman* pinned curling to the wall.
I saw her every time when I was small
– how she wept from all sides
of her fragmented Cubist face,
fierce the tears of his lover and muse,
grief-stricken woman of Guernica.
But I knew she was you
who'd *had it up to the neck* with him
and why I was round here anyway
with my friend wickedly telling me
the doors were a deadly poisonous paint
that we must dare lick and see.

# II. Tender Years

# Big Tod and Little Tod

for Saskia

*The siblings' cast off teddy bears*
*are slumped on granny's attic chair*

Big Tod always stayed at home. Little Tod
in tartan shorts came to school with me.

I thrashed him on the iron bed, showing off and more –
his head came off, sawdust over the dormitory floor.

I cried for killing the thing I loved
and knowing my mother could not repair.

At home Big Tod, tall as a child,
was Mummy's age in animal years,

which linked the day he was passed down,
already tatty, by a perfumed French hand
from the back of Daddy's Bedford van …

We brushed the scant yellow fur, threadbare skin
of our absent father. Made him a new felt ear,
reset the glass eye that hung by a thread.

The others: Sick Tiger, Jill doll, Pyjama Monkey,
stayed in his arms for a generation.

Little Tod, head sewn back on by a kind sister,
wore a scarf to hide his lack of neck,
and now never leaves my sock drawer.

While Big Tod himself has moved north
to live outside the walls of Stirling Castle.

# Summer of 1960

So I came to this town and met the teacher
who had married my real mother. Frank
fed my kitten sardines, blew smoke rings
to the ceiling, had a gold tooth worth money.

We cut a bamboo rod in his garden,
got fishing tackle at Miss Baker's;
walked a long hot road to the river,
fast and peat brown, banks thick with balsam.

There was nowhere to cast or sit down,
no bites either, not like daddy's canal
where anglers landed razor-teeth pike in the rain
and I held on to my other mother's hand.

Then we bought seedlings from the nursery,
a clump of lettuces that would flop at first,
biennial wallflowers to flower next year;
his earth was cloddy, not raked to a fine tilth.

Mrs O, yellow-fanged, came to tea. She wore a brooch
at her throat and had given him his bachelor digs.
Two sisters were arriving on different trains,
our mother was somewhere, not in the kitchen.

We collected one sister, then another,
sat down for broken biscuits which 'taste the same' –
ah, there she is pouring, trembling with the full teapot,
while reunited siblings ride their trikes in the yard.

We walked to the pond with pink and blue nets.
Rough boys fished for perch and thick-lipped tench,
smoking and laughing and breaking frogs' legs,
their cruel voices breaking.

We waded away, upstream in our pants
through weed and gassy mud, scooping
sticklebacks, minnows, grotesque bullheads
for their short-lived journey home in a jar.

Everyone went to fetch the car,
mother in her heels managed the stony track,
past the Miss Hoopers bent double in their garden.
I hauled the garage doors open, smelt petrol inside,

helped crank up his pre-war Morris Eight –
three of us in the back on cracked leather seats
in the only car that leaked. Picnic abandoned,
the rain dripped through our canvas roof.

Reaching home we'd forgotten the key.
Nothing for it but for me to shin the wall, break in.
I was small enough to worm through a window
head first: disastrous outing ends in triumph.

She read *Doctor Dolittle* for my story –
the emptiness came and she had to guess:
Is it school? Full boarding? Missing your father?
I nodded and burst.

But Frank was there with pads and chalks.
I drew the mountains on the moon, rockets.
We all of us drew something that first holiday
as we watched him take on the cooking –

fish fingers and skinless sausages, Angel Delight.
Rock buns, Vic sponge and fudge. Toff apples.
He even had a bash at candy floss:
we all learn by our mistakes.

Then the golden rod buzzed with bees,
summer was gone because it can't go on.
We filled the Box Brownie viewfinder
and he was driving me back to school.

# God Be With You Till We Meet Again

The last hymn of term, we sang it fast,
savagely, eliding the words, filled with
the warm shiver of holiday time.

In the dorm we sang and whistled
*One more day in this old dump*
*and we'll be home tomorrow.*

She wasn't in the car when they came,
she'd gone back in. Doors without handles
like police cars, upstairs windows barred.

We drove out to Tone Vale, missed *Z Cars.*
Gravel crunch, shaved lawns and yew,
miles of squeaky green corridor.

She was leant against the bedstead
in her smart black and white jacket,
dark glasses at the ready.

*Hey, you're supposed to take me out!*
(I will always be thirty years younger.)

We walked with her in the perfect grounds,
over a plank bridge to the patients' zoo
to nestle up with her, have our fill of her.

But Frank was calling from the bridge,
apple dumplings for supper, not for her.
She pleaded. *Not long*, his fierce whisper.

Time to go now, we must we must,
For me the country lanes back to school.
God be with you till we meet again.

# A Pink Nose

Anxious the tip of her nose should go pink,
she dabbed at it in the front seat,
then with pout and moue of glossed lips
I saw her reach for the fearful sunglasses.
'It's raining, Mum.'
'I know. My head.'
The alarm word *migraine*
and far-off place she would be sent.

You sent cards, so many snow scenes
cars, ships and aeroplanes.
They don't say much, tend to fuss,
yet I treasure the ones I've kept.
I just want you to know that,
just wish I could believe you are there.

# Migraine poem

For me: the onset's a cloud,
a muzz about the head
that waits in the cave as you wake.

It hasn't decided yet,
might fade when you move about,
splash water on your meek face.

Or a kind of hell that takes all day to come on.

You're acutely tuned
to this shift of internal weather,
Siberian wind that burns in summer,
shrills in winter
just behind the left eye
(first point on the meridian
for the acupuncture needle).

Now the start proper –
pulse, pound, pierce,
edge of elation, dread;
light scintillates through the curtain crack,
oh branch-squeak on the window glass,
fingernail scrape. Nausea. Thirst.
Please stop eating in my ear!
Every crunch, slurp and chew I hear.

I'll take you on, family curse
passed from grandfather I never knew,
through a mother I only sometimes knew
for whom Maria Callas once shattered
a wine glass in the darkened bedroom.
On the radio Gene Pitney grates.
Turn him off. Off!

Resistance is futile, it will wait,
return tomorrow if need be. It will out.
You take the drugs, grateful, lower
this crazy sparking head to cool pillow
for sleep of oblivion through the evening.

At three a.m. a few stars linger,
hunger drives you to the kitchen:
the comfort of a banana,
robin song in the neighbour's lilac.
Morning arrives with caution.

# Smusty Bowder

after *Hideous Kinky* by Esther Freud

A sign at the tea-table to meet after
for middle sister's special game.
*Oompah oompah stick it up yer jumper.*
'Do the eye thing,' she says
and my left eyebrow shoots up, lid quivers
genetically, ancestrally.
I flare my nostrils for good measure
and my grey-eyed sis laughs her head off.
That was enough.
We had the language, clicked:
*Clack. Gog. Smusty. Bowder.*

# Hard and Soft Centres

He went for the Whole Nut, Montelimar,
she the Cherry Cup, Vanilla Cream.

He had the spartan black kitchen chair,
she an upholstered one for her bum.

The children of Sparta were left out on the hill,
our garden's planted with sweet-scented flower.

Looking closer, his begonias and asters are harder
than her forget-me-nots, sweet williams

but they compromise on roses. Scent again:
Mme Alfred Carrière to Zéphirine Drouhin.

We pooled our pocket money needily,
hunted high and low for the perfect box of chocolates

half milk, half plain. Unless it was all a dream.

# The French Casserole

No dream, it strikes a rock in the grass,
breaks clean in half: two clay pieces.
But desolation hits the morning dew,
the *cucoo-cu-cucoo* of August woods;
our special camp fire by the river
burns on for nothing.

On holiday with our father,
he's still in his pyjamas
when I burst into the bedroom to tell.
He went so quiet,
seemed he'd never come back,
an upset too great
for me to understand.
Unforgivable, he meant.

Irreplaceable, brought back
from Provence with my mother,
that part of him I couldn't know.
Done now. No way back. No glue
can fix the fucking French casserole.
No words explain our mother of breakfasts
of dawn-gathered mushrooms from the hill
me and my sisters were cooking him.

Or skip back to another time,
his wild teatimes by the same river:
new mother's indoors fixing her bikini,
emerging to swim in the turgid weir pool
in the close insect air of high summer
down in the valley of wasps,
burnt jam tart and laughter.

# Frank's Haybox

From over his *Manchester Guardian*
he said we should cook with a haybox:
one of Granny's tea chests would do,
stuffed with newspaper and a tight lid.
'Start the casserole in the usual way,
then put in the box in the cellar
to braise twelve hours or more
for the family Sunday dinner.'

Haybox cooking came from the war.
The Van Gogh boots mother loved
(used for still lifes at school)
were his army ones from Sinai '45.
His garden spade of dark iron
looked just as time-worn. And the car
I mocked, confusing need with style,
forgetting his teacher's salary.

Gran, born before the other war,
approved mightily of haybox cooking.
She knew a thing or two about thrift:
the ten-shilling note poked into your mitt
never increased from fifty pence.
In nylon housecoat done up with clothes pegs
she fought to the end her daughter's excess,
her bloody jumping jack flash.

You can live, Frank told us, incredulous
at lunch, on five new pence a day:
on cabbage dumplings, water and lemon.
He was only being theoretical
but the depth of his thrift took Mum's breath away.
Goaded, defiant, she went out to the shops
and bought a dozen geraniums,
deep carmine through salmon to icing pink.

# Old Master

I found it in the attic, turned to the wall:
a small oil of muted tones, impasto
deftly built with strokes of palette knife

in an antique frame without glass:
View of the Tuileries from a high window,
white Sacré Coeur on a distant hill.

*Your father did that years ago –*
still the awed tone reserved for him
which only fogs me more – *Have it.*

From the time of Orlando
the marmalade cat, the French nanny,
the van they crisscrossed France in.

Thrilled to discover a bit more of my father,
I nailed up the painting in my room
with my Dylan and Leonard Cohen.

# Shagging Fields of Home

Hey, the May weather's great in our small town. Boys and girls are out in the high street, bikes propped against the Chippy window or thrown on the pavement wheels spinning. Down at the ponds a couple are fishing; he has his shirt off to show his pecs and tattoos; her straps are off milky shoulders while she suns herself, smokes a roll-up; he wants her but she can't today. An unlucky spaniel must keep fetching the stick its owners throw again, while the ducks watch and quack, and a mute swan speculates from the opposite bank. Parked buggies and strollers are empty. The path runs down to fields. Some follow the river past a sluice, through a tunnel under the main line. Well-used, filled with echoes and graffiti – then shattering din of the London train. Raised voices outside. He wants her to come lie in the long grass. She says there are thistles. They can use his coat. He's still pleading, she dangles her legs over the water.

# Seedlings

These springs they grip him,
father of one, step-parent of three
he watches them all come through.
Home from work, with Ma still in bed
and before going to make the tea,
he goes to the greenhouse
to water the trays of tomatoes,
cucurbits and capsicums,
his nursery of half-hardies,
her rose-scented geraniums.

Thank you, Frank,
I was well looked after,
fed on bananas and milk,
manna for the coming weeks
of my first city bedsit.
Yet your letter to me
was all of thanks.

# III. Funeral Blues

i.m. Anne Wild 7.12.1923–5.3.1998

# Evening, Early March

Rain rain, still falling on the pond
brimming now, pellucid, green;
I can scarcely fathom how much
rain has fallen these last few days.
The herring-bone bricks are washed clean,
the green bamboo sways and grows;
see blackbird comes, cool and sharp,
eye fixing me as he dips in the pool
where primroses and baby's tears
crowd in from every side. All of this,
and the nodding host of tête-à-têtes
we planted by the grave, conspire
to bring on an ache in spring
however strong the resolve.

# The Directions

Turn left out of your road
and left again, all the way.
Go left at every roundabout
for a hundred miles, I have found.

I'm glad you are going just now,
West Country blustery, narcissi in bud;
take good shoes and all your memories.
When you arrive at the town centre,
the lights, grim town hall – remember
the day the big end on the Vanguard
went with such a clatter and smoke
we nearly died in the back seat!

– you can take your first right now
down Waterloo Road to the house:
see how the wayfaring tree has filled out,
the edges of the bricks grown softer,
her white dressing-table still in the window.

Or if going straight to the cemetery,
it's over at the lights and one last left
down deep-cut lane to the open gate.
Take the cinder path of *The Stranger Song*
we always sang – past dreary marble
chippings, shows of perpetual flowers,
and across the grass, dear sister,
sharp at the first cut of the year.

# The Interment

Where cinder path turns under the cypress
a man in black waits patiently for us.
Casket of solid oak, brass fittings – size
of the box of fish knives we never used.
I don't know what to do. Kiss it now
or later, when she goes in with Gran?
Mr Fudge holds firm with his large hands –
with our tinkers' blood, her mother said
we might do anything, seize Anne's ashes
and rush away through the hallowed ground,
leap the ditch and rusty barbed wire,
cross a field of astonished brindled cows,
run right up the thorn and bracken hill
to finally reach the town Monument
where we got the keys when we were small;
and climb that immensely tall spiral stair
to the highest part of the land round here,
all forgiven, forgotten as we cling to the box,
open the lid and throw her ashes to the wind.
Then we would need to look around for wings.

# 1998

Those quiet watercolours
tending to sombre, raw
umber, sienna, Payne's grey
churchy dark though he was no Christian
or like dark carpets, perhaps Islamic
marvellously intricate geometry
of a slowly turning mandala
but no god there either
he simply made his modest squares
with steady hand and size zero sable
year on year, home from teaching
evenings at the kitchen table
the children-filled weekends

This burst of colour
expanded, circular, rectangular
orange, cobalt, magenta
star-spangled banner
bull's-eye and firework
nods to other gods
Kandinsky, Klee, Gris

# Stinker

Don't be such a swine,
close your decorator's eye
to the peeling paintwork,
smudge of mould around the sink,
spongy sill that hints of rot –
see those lovely Victorian tiles she kept.
Oh roller towel on the scullery door
was always stinker poo-poo wee-wee.

Dry your hands on your trousers,
don't mention sanitation,
hygiene or new regulation.
Spare a thought for years ago
out here in the back loo,
the nightmare of the call in the night.
Leave Joan Sutherland to caterwaul upstairs
while he paints in his late exuberance.

I sniffed at the crusted yellow
carton of clotted cream,
looked for a date on the lid
while they dolloped it on the tart.

# Mother's Day Anniversary

We wake tenderly, have our coffee in bed,
there are lilies *For Mom* on the kitchen table;
we flip pancakes and feed the ravenous mog.
Then drive to a plant centre, to buy a shell-pink
Japanese quince for both your mum and mine
to plant in view of the cooker and sink.
For our special meal we have fish and rice,
watch Angela Gheorghiu sing from *Butterfly*,
follow her home to the painted wooden
mountain churches of northern Romania
and exquisite plainsong flows over the room
and I rejoin with my creator,
lay her to rest once again,
then get on with the washing up.

# The Photographic History

She left him in peace of a kind.
He turned the house into a shrine,

everywhere her framed photographs:
Diana look, angled, downcast; the laugh

in Mary Quant skirt with bouffant hair;
that loud loud hat in the window chair;

heady stuff for us, his dark-room craze,
'a record of her glamorous phase.'

Then fewer sittings, just one or two –
she'd put on weight, had the summer blues,

You're glum as a dog on Mogodon, Mum,
on your Valium, Valium, Valium.

She came back; laughed again; filled out. Teeth came out.
No more, she said, leant on the sun dial for support.

Soon she'd be stabbing white-sticked down the road
in the last picture of the record he made.

It's still a mystery, he murmured at the crem,
our man of absolute atheism.

He still gets his frames from the charity shop,
keeps himself busy with the backlog.

# The Blue Armchair

Sometimes on a Saturday afternoon
when the others are shopping in town
I'm drawn to the matinee movie.
Telly on, feet up – I become her
with her memories of light.
I mean,
my closed eyes, my clenched eyes
– sunlight streaming through a window bay
to the saggy blue armchair surrounded by bags –
are *your* unseeing eyes, and that late
smacking sound of your pill-dry mouth.
Then I'm asleep, dreaming different things –
of your portfolio under the bed, the figures
and faces, farm animals, wild flowers,
none of which came to much –
and they come in, wake Dad with a laugh,
put on sport or a quiz
and I get up to cook the supper.
I like that brief time
when I am you, you are me,
between what has been and what will come.
It happens more often now.

# IV. Rouge et Noir

# Flout

KEEP OUT in thick white paint on a gate
is an invitation, bull or not, an obstruction.
Rules are made to be. That way's quicker.

And the red man at the lights beckons –
I hardly pause, step over the kerb, forget my friend
who looked left in Paris and was hit by a bus.

KEEP OFF THE GRASS: we kicked off our shoes,
stepped over the ivy-covered chain in the park
to walk hand in hand, free in love.

Further back, Grandpa's large preprandial
in the White Hart was *Stuff and nonsense! Jump in!*
From the scented leather of his Daimler

we watched him perform a five-point turn
on that straight stretch of the A4
as the distant red Mazda ploughed into us.

(He asked *his own son* to perjure himself
about the drink, Dad still protested decades later.)

You lived there so long, Ma, they put up a sign:
NO SKATEBOARDING £500 FINE
on our silver lamppost outside the house.

The book from the bottom of the teetering pile
I know will be the one I want to read next.

# Misfit

She watched them on the aerials and wires,
sun-glanced feathers, bronze and ultramarine.
From her bed they were part of the all day scene,
pops, clicks and whistles that never tired.

One of these bright sparks she got to know,
a misfit with a curved sickle bill,
urchin from the bottom of the hill,
part jewelled exotic, part Chaplin crow.

When her eyes began to cloud and grey,
this rooftop Topol became a friend;
bird and radio kept her 'on the mend'
while her visual world fell away.

She kept me updated with calls for a year
on her Mozart starling with malformed beak;
worried through winter how it managed to eat
until one spring morning it disappeared.

# Glaucoma and Naming the Cat

Clink of tile, click of latch, Frank's gone out;
puss still without a name is noisily washing.
How is it this morning? Are they even open?
Reaching over to the scalloped table edge,
she has become Sphinx under the lamp.

Now jumps across to headbutt, lick me
with her rough little tongue, make puddings.
Actually, it's worse, a mist in both now,
with light only at the periphery.
Puss rolls over for a tummy rub

till claws flex and stab, back legs pummel.
With the good one going, it's getting pretty dull
around here. Thank you God for the radio, she's saying
while sweeping the counterpane's empty space.
He promised he would only be an hour.

Soon he'll come and arm in arm with her new white stick
they'll parade as far as the Methodist on the corner
where HE WILL SAVE YOU shrieks from a yellow poster ...
Now where was she? Ah, Côte d'Azur in spring, mimosa
and the actor mother of a long ago hubby ...

Squeak of the unoiled front gate,
rattle of catflap in the distant kitchen,
a loose hall tile, creaky stair tread ...
and she springs to her place on the bed:
Thomasina or Sheba or Helen Keller!

# Disappeared

The card from Harry always came.
'Here it is! I was wondering ...'
She gave him pride of place on the mantel.
His woodblocks and linocuts stretched back
beyond my life to Brighton Art School
during the war, and they were saved –
I have a pouncing cat from Christmas '48.
They stayed up so long you stopped seeing them,
then they ceased.

She met Llewelyn on the Level
at the back of the art school
every Friday afternoon without fail –
we loved to hear of our mother with her
Welsh communist, aged seventeen,
between the fire-watching and ARP.
One day her sweetheart wasn't there.
She waited every Friday for a year.

# Before Ikea

Imagine our mother on a trip to Ikea,
she was always game.
Steady, Ma, mind the kerb.
Remember the hole in the road at Notting Hill …
*Carnival, the rhythm, the drumming, Dad in Brazil.*
Mount the stairs to the new store
with a doyenne of the sales –
all new, her grown children excited too.
But feet are killing her, the drugs parch her –
we go straight to the cafeteria.
*Ooch that's better. Hit the spot.*
Have a lie down, Mum.
Like an elderly dowager mog
she chooses a bed in the showroom, shoes on …
Ikea's here but not her.
The right time for me was too late for her.
It's a hard thing to coincide with a parent.
Half-blind, she was already taking to her bed,
the last place of refuge.


## Oh Mum's Vintage

At the back of her wardrobe
a full bottle of scotch – Teacher's –
came to light a decade after she died.


## Found Postcard

'I was going to write to you
in our favourite garden centre
after a huge vegetarian lunch
but this enormous spayed tabby
jumped on my lap and stayed.'

# Marmalade Making

Now is the time in dark of winter
to put on Fado, settle at the table
with a board and sharp knife to quarter the fruit,
the unwaxed Sevilles and lemon,
squeeze the juice, scrape the pith, save the pips,
slice the peel into short fine lines,
fingers tight on the pitted skin,
sinking the blade in time after time,
the keen aroma freed in a spray
as her voice swells through your head.

# The Portuguese Photograph

'The people look so nice, dark eyes,
olive skin,' she says and asks for a gin,
takes off her shoes, wiggles stockinged toes,
seems to be beside me, strapped in.

I feel good too, like a baby
fed and burped by the careful cabin crew.
Aren't we lucky to have the gap-toothed one,
a fairy in dark blue.

At the Central Hotel, the photos spread,
all sepia snaps: toddler with her nurse,
*the house with a boulder in the garden*,
a part address in pencil on the reverse.

'Just to sit in the cafés,' she'd murmur,
'with my mother in her silks and straw hat,
Teddy home from the bank, smoking his pipe;
my nurse Bedí always wore black like that.'

Now she's toiling up Lisbon's sheer hills,
keeping on with her incessant chatter;
she feels for an adult's leathery hand,
puffs all the way to the funicular.

'The beggars are all still here,' she protests,
'the hideous and deformed still by the cathedral.'
We walk on the rippling black and white mosaic
that trips her, doesn't suit her heels at all.

Pavements later we chew octopus salad
in a café with a soundtrack of Abba.
'The colours, canaries,' the child in her cries.
'Beat of Brazil, Bossanova! The house is in Sintra!'

Our small train climbs to Sintra's tiled station,
the glorious Eden of Byron's *Childe Harold*;
through forested hills, up dizzying steps,
we follow the path to a Moorish stronghold.

Songbirds and mynahs sing in their cages,
a whitethroat, migrating, replies from the trees;
morning glory drapes the gates of a *quinta*
which could be the one, she falls to her knees.

'Bedí was here. I begged. She spared the goose
but killed the snake. We left her behind
to sail in the white ocean liner
taking Daddy to hospital in England this time.'

Higher and higher the climb, now after
one flight of steps in particular,
where she sat with Bedí in the sun
outside the fabulous Palácio da Pena.

# Teddy

Shell shock hell in the trenches. 23.3.18, shot in the back at the Battle of St Quentin. The wound healed but not his battle dreams. Nerves shredded, 'fagged out', the bank in Lisbon returned him to a hospital in England: The Maudsley, Haywards Heath Asylum, Graylingwell; primitive electric-shock treatment of the time. In 1935 he bought a bungalow in Rottingdean with Granny Betty, and hung on at the bank. They finally let him go, sacked the unreliable, battle-dreaming Captain Wild. He lived at home with his only child; her mother worked to the bone to keep them from the work house. He walked the South Downs, swam with the Brighton and Hove Shiverers between the piers. The years of unemployment, continuing illness, war pension appeals – until his suicide in 1951.

In the photo proud Anne, towel under arm, is striding with her daddy to the pool.

# Soup of Antidepressants

Oh Anne, you ate them, bathed in them:
Diazepam, Lithium, Librium, Amitryptyline,
Imipramine, Anafranil, Tofranil, Ativan,
even Largactyl for your episodes;
and Prozac came, Fluoxetine to Citalopram –
now in every ocean to the seabed
we make a soup the shellfish can't eat.
Limpets loosen grip on the primeval rock.

# Yehudi

I opened a bottle of wine
and soon left cooking behind
as I tripped the Light Fantastic
down the garden path in the dark
in my old London clogs,
in a rush of Jellicle delight.

Blue moon craning over rooftops,
dims even the street lights now.
There's alley cat in the day's heat,
creaking cedar of this shed
and the ghost of her stirs in the hammock:
*Yehudi, Yehudi Menuhin.*

# Fig Therapy

for SW

On a southern roof terrace
among black redstarts, oriole calls,
your paintings now from photographs,
Dionysian, the Rhône red wine and figs.

Their soft and purple-dusted skin
split open with a fingernail
to outrageous sticky seed;
half each we always shared.

And sweeter still the golden ones
found on the high, dry Coiron;
reaching over a tarmac edge
we hoiked them in with sticks.

Back home to dewy mornings, we watch
the slow ripening in England.

# Morning Glory

You asleep in a henna storm,
sunlight drawn around the curtain,
I clamber over into September.

Clear skies again, and today's glories –
bees scrambling into the silky trumpets
that will bloom only for a morning.

We crumple too by evening, gone
the blue midnights, afternoons of curtains drawn.
But we still have each start of day

and eyes closed I can still hear Anne's cry of joy
to all the ipomoea of her Atlantic childhood,
*Ooh the morning glory.*

# Dawn Chorus

Listen, I'm in the buttoned armchair,
the green velvet one that he upholstered,
with your letters spread on my knee.

We've had tea, been up to town,
seen the best church in Devon.

I was out on the Common, 4.30 am,
as I aim to each spring,
this time in time.

I was there when they began,
down where the path turns and dips –
that equinoctial tide of birdsong.

In a hawthorn, two young thrushes
practised their simple repetitions;
among garden warbler, blackcap, wren.

You must be there, Ma, at the beginning,
when the first one sings and the echo comes,
another and another.

Sing with me now.

# Dragonfly

Late, late in the sultry afternoon,
gift of a gorgeous crimson peony
on the garden table, bottle of Tempranillo
in fine gold mesh like a stocking unopened.
We touched miracle embryo lemons,
looked for figs under rough-nap leaves;
the great hawker dragonfly we'd rescued
from our feline rustled its wings on the path.

And in the field of brilliant orange California
poppies, I crouch to collect ripe brown
seed pods curled back ready to catapult;
snap them off and tip – the future –
into an envelope to send you
to sow on your sunbaked terrace at home.

# Rouge et Noir

Then gazing out on a grey dawn
the Oriental poppy has burst open –

gash of scarlet that still shocks,
slashed at the hem, scissor-nipped,
all else in the garden eclipsed
like the frills of a nightdress once.

I'm pulled back there, outside
to raise a great nodding head,
black-dusted anemone arms,
stoop to bury my face in the musk.

I brought her a stem, it lay ablaze
on the white kitchen counter.
Then we saw a man cycling, didn't we,
a rose gripped between his teeth.

Seems I must repeat every year
this film of the poppy's theatre
from the *coup de foudre* of that summer.

# Olive Tee-shirt

I clung to the side, the edge of the shelf
but over I went and I fell so far
that when I awoke and opened my eyes,
felt with my hand, I couldn't believe
you weren't there on the pillow –
I left you barefoot in your gown,
drove away through the yellow midnight town.

You teased me, said
there's no such thing as chemistry,
we learn what the other needs is all
and where's the alchemy in that?
I said what about the knowing within
five minutes of meeting?

And it isn't only the ground-heaving, earth-bending, whitewater rafting.
It's in the sweet little, endless little tugs and touches and after-kisses,
the honey talk, sugar whisper, glued together.

No other way to put it, love is a cliché
we long to get back to
as we muddle through the days.

In a cupboard of dark salty olives,
in a brew of fresh coffee.
In the balance of you on me,
legs stretched to infinity,
we fit is all – physics equals chemistry.

You're on the phone now, somewhere
dancing down the hall
in your embroidered dressing gown.

I'll keep my sweaty tee-shirt on,
wear the scent of you close to my heart,
won't wash it until you come back.
I have this message buzzing around:
welcome home, my love, I've dug up
all the Spanish bluebells in your garden.

# Vertigo Outside the Festival Hall

On a damp November night
leant against the parapet wall,
you could so easily –
just like that paper cup, dance
down the slanting stone
on a mere breath of wind
to the very edge – fall.

These fantastic notions of topping oneself,
feeling so bad you can't even phone.
The most awful thing you've ever done,
*you must atone* –
ideas you've had before: wedged
in the clifftop some glorious sunset,
full bottle of scotch in your hand
and the tide turns …
or the noose one
where your own arm is the gallows
that haul you back and up.

Like her war-wrecked father
who used a beam in the garage.
*Terrible business*, the neighbour said,
*the girl found a drop of his blood …*
We only knew she ran from the room
whenever there was a hanging
in the Westerns we watched on TV.

Here, on the surface at least,
this vertigo seems to stem
from the coccyx vestigial tail,
spread down from there to the knees,
while sending a shiver up the spine
with the instruction to lean out more:
*Go on. Land by the dosser and his dog.*

Your hand grips the lip of stone,
the pitted wrecked surface closes in;
lichens that grow a millimetre a year
come into focus in marvellous detail;
concert lights stream from the hall behind,
and your feet begin to rise –

you levitate outside the double doors,
ready to fly in and show them all
the greatest show the world's ever seen
*no, not now… all a mistake … unpolished shoes.*

There, it's over. Won't trouble for a while.

# Donovan's Socks

for HL

'Years ago, we waited hours outside the Savoy,
only got Long John Baldry's that night.

So we two girls walked from Muswell Hill
to Hatfield, Herts for Donovan's autograph.

He isn't in, he's at a gig, said his Mom
but we could see his room if we liked.

Would we! *Colours, Hurdy Gurdy, Universal Soldier*;
she rummaged and gave us a pair of his socks.

The Peace banner on his wall was rubbish
so we made him another at school.'

# A Dylan Tall Story

for P

My friend was waiting for a bus
when along Crouch End Road
came the man himself.
'How's it going?' he said
and Bob looked kind of strange,
said he'd been for tea at Dave Stewart's
house, only Dave wasn't there.
His missus invited him in,
they sat in the front room
with bone china and Garibaldis
and talked of the Never Ending Tour.
Her Dave was such a fan,
they went to see his workshop –
Zimmerman all over the wall.
My friend, another Dylan nut,
can't get it out of his head
that Bob went to tea
with the wrong Mrs Stewart.


## Interview on the Cusp of Fame

Suck your glasses, Bob.
What?
Suck 'em. Put the arm in the corner of your mouth.
Christ, man, what do you *want* with me? *You* suck my glasses.

# The Fisherman's Daughter

How far from all that now:
Kujukuri
out on the ninety-nine mile
beach, the catch that came in,
a bag of tiny silver fish
left on Obāchan's step.
And the poet set to clean them
under icy tap of winter;
she arranged raw slivers on a plate,
brought bowls of rice and miso, withdrew.
She doesn't eat fish any more.
As a girl she ran to the boats:
*They grabbed a flapping fish for me,*
*snapped off the head, skinned it in one,*
*rinsed it in the sea.*
It tasted of the sea of Japan.

   *Far across the world*
   *we see the same moon tonight*
   *on your beach and mine*

Obāchan   little Japanese grandmother, often used affectionately for mother

# Wonderful World

Dizzy in the swarming town centre
sit with your bags by a grizzled character
with their Down syndrome daughter.

Readibus enters the shopping arena –
a council steed in shining armour
dropping off oldies like a dispenser.

*… hear babies cry, watch them grow,*
some busker outside Marks & Spencer
croons Mum's song over and over.

You see the ribbed navy-blue sweater
she once bought Frank in Jaeger
that amply outlasted her.

On the next bench, legs akimbo
kids loll and smoke reefer,
share cans of Coke or lager.

Now a refugee voice from Somalia
wails from her heart with the busker
by the big bank on the corner.

Nip in there for a biro and paper.
Can't phone her, no credit on your Nokia,
you can only wait here for her.

# Flipflop Tiger

My Leo on her fiftieth birthday,
a rusty mane may she never shear.
Orange teeshirt and painted beads
embrace me in the hall – and then
out into the crazy heat and rain
to slip and slide in flip-flops
dogged down the road to school
with all the other stretched mums
on the run, this last week of term.
Here comes the sun.

# Don't you just hate it
# when they shout at their kids

the girl with the hoop earrings says to her friend
on a bench in the shiny new shopping mall.
I heard it too, saw a young mum
at the end of her tether on the marble floor,
bags of shopping tipping the buggy, a bawling child.
I don't know what's going on
but a shout like that burns me like ice –
*What goes on at home?*
                        It has cut through
to those girls too, all heels and blusher,
chat and chewing gum, on the phone
from their mid-town station Friday afternoon.
And I'm so glad I could hug them
as I move off down the now hollow hall,
leaving mother and child at dodgems on the floor.

# Mother Spleenwort

I hardly went out the back
that winter, and Marjorie's fern
was all but forgotten,
unwatered since Christmas.

She showed me its ancestor,
New Zealand '68,
the great fern that had grown
from a bulbil smuggled in her handbag.

New bulbils, tiny, pale green,
perched along the older fronds,
ready to be dibbed into the earth,
were like the babies she couldn't have.

The last time I saw her in the dayroom
feet up on an ottoman, 95, brothers
all gone, *not much point in carrying on*,
she enquired again who I was.

My fern became a dozen more.
I passed them on, they lived and died,
and this may be the last.
I drip-feed the dried-up thing with rainwater.

# In the House of the Deaf

The note pinned to the door:
RING BOTH BELLS LOUDLY
but we have a key.
He waves from her chair, shouts:
*Good of you both …*
TURN IT DOWN, FRANK! Is your aid in?
*Digital, yes. Won't go any higher.*
We'll get you an ear trumpet!
which has him chortling.
Sorry to be late. The M5.
*Funnily enough I can pick up*
*almost everything Ali says.*
Just hears what he wants to hear,
she always said under her breath,
I tell him under mine.

CRICKET, FRANK!
It's on so loud from India,
you could it hear next door.
Up the walls to the bedrooms,
the loo, attic unseen for years,
and down in the cellar's glistening coal,
ancient demijohns of dandelion wine
once of much interest to his wife.

Her connivance in the steamy
scullery: Don't you get it,
the euphoria, family curse?
She laughed then, on top of it.
I laughed with her, shrugged it off.

Wrestling with back door bolts,
we venture into a jungle garden.
*That's nothing. You should see Elwin's,*

he calls. Elwin next door
fell backwards down his cellar steps,
was lucky to break only a bone.
Hasn't been in his garden since.

In the night a fresh burst of radio
*loud enough to wake the dead!*
from somewhere in the house.
It's still dark when Sunday Worship
filters up the stairs. Caught religion, Frank?
*The pre-set comes on*, he grins
okay this morning
as we prepare to leave.

# Like the Man from St Ives

*Tap creak, tap creak*
shopping trolley up the hall –
it always had a slope.

Now he tackles the stairs,
the up down, down up
long day of it.

*All part of the daily dozen,*
the *A to B and back.*
We call it his Himalaya,
climbed twice (including a nap),
while hoping from afar
he left his stick at the top.

Four wheels again, out
for afternoon push.
Negotiate the front step,
then it's plain to George Street.

Quick quick, he wants it,
*all over in ten minutes*
like Anne's friend 'St Ives'
on his last trip to the wine shop.

And don't we all *when it comes*
only not for the one we love.

# The Shed

In the end it's down to me
to dismantle what I once put up.
So many cobwebs left inside here
before I can even begin –
and how they grab at you,
bring mischief, his sense of fun: grape scissors,
the garden fork handle, mouldy holdall holding what?
Smell the catty cedar, tobacco tin of galvanised nails,
weigh in with a great coil of wire, that pulley system,
find the cabin hooks and vine eyes, nuts and bolts of him,
All these remainders made their way out here:
a Georgian window frame, cottage stable door;
Alzheimer aluminium and Anne's lead-glazed pots again,
odd lead flashing salvaged for his waterfall.
All these things must we shed?

Now the bones of it:
the door, walls, roof and floor.
No one comes out to help
but they wave and advise,
friendly enough from a distance,
this other strand of my father's family –
still it goes on: from a different mother
can never be forgotten.
We gaze into the shell of his leaving,
lucky grin and pipe smoke of him,
bluster and sense of occasion
which would turn this into a celebration,
something for us all
at this grand moment of demolition.

# Kindness to a Stranger

She finds it floundering in a puddle,
brings it home, gives it a shoe box,
warms it on a chair beside the stove.

She takes a soft-bristled brush,
strokes the feathers of back and breast,
intuitively, inventively.

The rain stops. She steps outside
and opens her cupped hands.
The young swift flies, joins the others
screaming over the town gardens.

# Baby Sitting

for Nevie

One two three, says Finny-fin fish.
*Aye way away*, she sings.

Tinkling spring and silver wave,
waterfall and salmon spawn,

a *plethora* of eggs laid at dawn
in the same stream she was born –

*Way way*, she understands and likes this book.

*Ai Wei* Wei, you're a dissident Chinese artist!

Eyes hold me safe and near
while she's sat straight-backed on the floor

winter morning sun flooding in,
I have all the trust in the world.

Ma and Da have gone out without her,
slingless for the first time in her life.

They're away from the flat, Nevie!
*Way awah awawah wayyy.*

They're back! and Mum gets a whack for that,
finger-claw up her nose.

But a mother doesn't mind so much –
*wah away, awah-wah way.*

I will try to be there every time she calls
*Grandma, Grandda.*

Two Rivers Press has been publishing in and about Reading
since 1994. Founded by the artist Peter Hay (1951–2003),
the press continues to delight readers, local and further afield,
with its varied list of individually designed,
thought-provoking books.